BOOK BUDDIES

MORRISON | | hooks | ATWOOD)) YOUSAFZAI

T0182494

Doyle | | (SAPPHO) Le Guin)) | 0

bold,

Frank | L'ENGLE | (BRONTË) Lee | | |

((ANGELOU))

badass,

Wheatley | |

and
bookish

duopress

an imprint of ⑤ sourcebooks

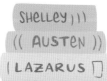

SHELLEY))) ((AUSTEN)) | LAZARUS |

women writers
make ~~history~~
HERSTORY

Bold CREATOR

Courageous

TRUTH-TELLER

brave inspirational

Spirited

provocative

LIFELONG LEARNER

Storyteller

RE-INVENTER

"A word after a word after a word is POWER."

—MARGARET ATWOOD

No black woman writer in this culture can write 'too much.' Indeed, no woman writer can write 'too much' . . .

NO WOMAN HAS WRITTEN ENOUGH.

—bell hooks

Find your voice.

Why did *bell hooks* lowercase her name?

To focus attention on her works, rather than on herself.

How did she choose her pen name?

Born Gloria Jean Watkins, bell hooks chose her pen name as a tribute to her grandmother, Bell Blair Hooks.

Can you match these women writers with their pen names?

George Sand

George Eliot

A. M. Barnard

Michael Field

Currer, Ellis, and Acton Bell

Edith Cooper and Katherine Bradley

Louisa May Alcott

Amantine Lucile Aurore Dupin

The Brontë sisters (Charlotte, Emily, and Anne)

Mary Ann Evans

(Turn the page for the answers!)

The pen is mightier than the sword

Answers

George Sand
Amantine Lucile Aurore Dupin

Currer, Ellis, and Acton Bell
The Brontë sisters (Charlotte, Emily, and Anne)

George Eliot
Mary Ann Evans

A. M. Barnard
Louisa May Alcott

Michael Field
Edith Cooper and Katherine Bradley

TRUTH-TELLER

The author of *Incidents in the Life of a Slave Girl*—a real documentation of the horrific conditions of slave life—was unknown until the 1980s. Although the book was accepted as nonfiction when it was published, *Incidents in the Life of a Slave Girl* was dubbed fictional by 20th-century critics. It wasn't until the 1980s that the truth came out, when a researcher discovered a trove of letters proving that **Harriet Jacobs** was the author and that the events were accurate.

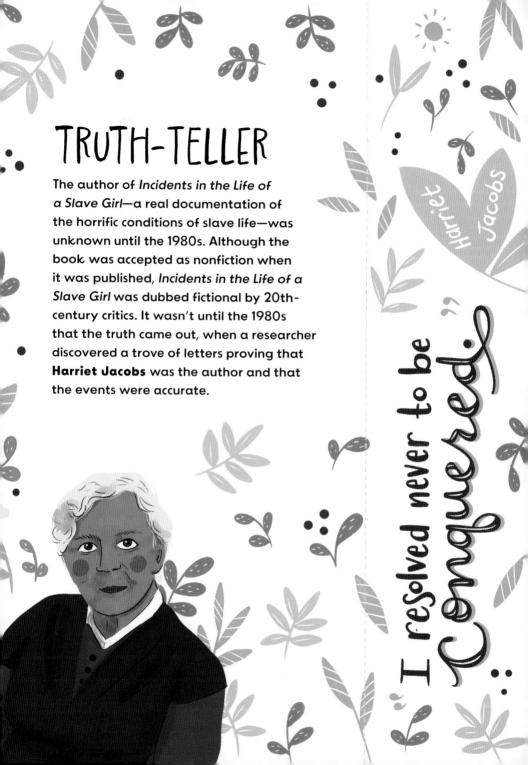

Harriet Jacobs

"I resolved never to be Conquered."

Further Reading

First-person accounts by heroic women:

The Diary of Anne Frank
by Anne Frank

Incidents in the Life of a Slave Girl
by Harriet Jacobs

***I Am Malala: The Girl Who Stood Up for
Education and Was Shot by the Taliban***
by Malala Yousafzai

The Unabridged Journals of Sylvia Plath
by Sylvia Plath

The Story of My Life
by Helen Keller

***Last Night I Dreamed of Peace:
The Diary of Dang Thuy Tram***
by Dang Thuy Tram

Dust Tracks on a Road
by Zora Neale Hurston

"Until we are all free, we are none of us free."

—Emma Lazarus

READ BOOKS, CHANGE THE WORLD.

Sneaky Reads

In the 16th century, book publishers who wanted to provide novels to women produced smaller, cheaper versions of books that could be easily snuck past the eyes of disapproving husbands.

Do you know the answers to these questions about banned books?

Which Pulitzer Prize–winning books have often been censored from schools?

Occult themes and offensive language are cited as reasons for banning which young adult classic?

Which best-selling memoir is one of the most-banned books of all time?

(Turn the page for the answers!)

BANNED book club

BE
FREE
To
Read!

Answers

To Kill a Mockingbird by Harper Lee and
The Color Purple by Alice Walker

A Wrinkle in Time by Madeleine L'Engle

I Know Why the Caged Bird Sings by
Maya Angelou

"Every time you pretend to be less than you are, you steal permission from other women to EXIST FULLY"

—Glennon Doyle

She is...

strong

fierce

brave

FULL OF FIRE

"YOU CANNOT BUY
THE REVOLUTION.
YOU CANNOT MAKE THE
REVOLUTION. YOU CAN
ONLY BE THE REVOLUTION.
It is in your Spirit,
OR IT IS NOWHERE."

—Ursula K. Le Guin, *The Dispossessed*

An Incomplete List of
Early Women Writers

ENHEDUANNA
Akkadian poet and high priestess of a temple in the city of Ur (in modern-day Iraq). Dubbed the "world's first author known by name."

SAPPHO
A Greek poet whose work has been mostly lost to time. Plato called her "the Tenth Muse." A type of poetic meter ("sapphic") bears her name.

RABI'A AL-'ADAWIYYA AL-QAYSIYYA
Sufi mystic and poet. Considered the first saint in the Muslim Sufi tradition.

MARIE DE FRANCE
A mysterious nun and French poet who lived in England in the 12th century.

PHILLIS WHEATLEY
Published a book of poetry in 1773—the first African American published author.

MARY WOLLSTONECRAFT
Author of *A Vindication of the Rights of Woman* (1792), a significant early feminist work. Died shortly after giving birth to her daughter, Mary (Shelley).

women writers make history

herstory

Literacy: A Long-Fought Battle

In the Middle Ages, nuns and religious figures were the women most likely to be literate. Hildegard von Bingen, Marie de France, and Margery Kempe are all examples of prolific women writers from that period. Some, like Julian of Norwich, used masculine pen names to write their own books and poems. Others have been lost to time and are now known only as Anonymous.

Piece of My Heart

Mary Shelley kept a gothic keepsake—the calcified heart of her husband (Percy Bysshe Shelley)—wrapped inside a copy of his poem "Adonais." His heart had not burned when he was cremated, so she carried it with her everywhere.

Frankenstein is widely considered the first science-fiction novel. Mary Shelley claimed it came to her in a "waking dream."

"*Beware,* FOR I AM *fearless* AND THEREFORE *powerful.*"

—Mary Shelley, *Frankenstein*

" Lock up your libraries if you like; but there is no gate, no lock, no bolt that you can set upon

THE FREEDOM OF MY MIND. **"**

—Virginia Woolf,
A Room of One's Own

"No need to
hurry.

No need to
sparkle.

No need to be
anybody but
oneself."

—Virginia Woolf,
*A Room
of One's Own*

Who was Virginia Woolf?

A pioneering modernist author who wrote novels, essays, and nonfiction that shaped modern feminist thought.

She founded the Hogarth Press with her husband, Leonard.

Woolf's novel *Orlando* was inspired by her great love for Vita Sackville-West.

Famous Authors Who
Overcame the Odds

Joan Didion was diagnosed with multiple sclerosis in her thirties.

Octavia Butler referred to herself as "a bit dyslexic" in several interviews.

Adrienne Rich was disabled due to severe arthritis—she wrote poems about physical pain.

Frida Kahlo lived with spina bifida and the aftereffects of polio and wore a full-body cast after a horrible trolley accident. Though she is most famous for her artistic work, she kept an illustrated diary that was published posthumously.

Agatha Christie had dysgraphia, which affects the ability to write.

Sometimes an **obstacle** is an **opportunity.**

"Literature is my Utopia."

—Helen Keller,
The Story of My Life

Match these dystopian novel titles to their setting.

The Giver	Panem
Who Fears Death	Jwahir
Parable of the Sower	The Community
The Hunger Games	Minnesota
Future Home of the Living God	The Republic of Gilead
The Handmaid's Tale	California

(Turn the page for the answers!)

NOLITE TE BASTARDES CARBORUNDORUM.

Answers

The Handmaid's Tale (Margaret Atwood)
The Republic of Gilead

The Giver (Lois Lowry)
The Community

Who Fears Death (Nnedi Okorafor)
Jwahir

Parable of the Sower (Octavia E. Butler)
California

The Hunger Games (Suzanne Collins)
Panem

Future Home of the Living God (Louise Erdrich)
Minnesota

If there's a book you really want to read, but it hasn't been written yet, *then you must write it.* "

—Toni Morrison

" YOU ARE YOUR *best* THING. "

—Toni Morrison

A Few Facts About
Toni Morrison

Published *The Bluest Eye,* her first novel, at age 39.

Her given name was Chloe. "Toni" was a nickname and her pen name, adopted after others had trouble pronouncing Chloe.

First African American to win a Nobel Prize in Literature.

One of the first Black editors at a publishing house (Random House), helping diverse authors establish themselves in a white male-dominated field.

Which of these women won a Nobel or Pulitzer Prize?

- ☐ Pearl S. Buck
- ☐ Willa Cather
- ☐ Jennifer Egan
- ☐ Elfriede Jelinek
- ☐ Jhumpa Lahiri
- ☐ Doris Lessing
- ☐ Gabriela Mistral
- ☐ Toni Morrison
- ☐ Alice Munro
- ☐ Herta Müller
- ☐ Wisława Szymborska
- ☐ Edith Wharton

(Check the back for the answers!)

Blaze your own trail.

All of them!

- → Pearl S. Buck: Nobel Prize

- → Willa Cather: Pulitzer Prize (*One of Ours*)

- → Jennifer Egan: Pulitzer Prize (*A Visit from the Goon Squad*)

- → Elfriede Jelinek: Nobel Prize

- → Jhumpa Lahiri: Pulitzer Prize (*Interpreter of Maladies*)

- → Doris Lessing: Nobel Prize

- → Gabriela Mistral: Nobel Prize

- → Toni Morrison: Nobel Prize, Pulitzer Prize (*Beloved*)

- → Alice Munro: Nobel Prize

- → Herta Müller: Nobel Prize

- → Wisława Szymborska: Nobel Prize

- → Edith Wharton: Pulitzer Prize (*The Age of Innocence*)

To Read Is to Rebel

Medical experts of the 19th century blamed novels for women's "hysteria," a term used to write off inconvenient emotions, or behaviors deemed socially unacceptable, as a "disorder" of the uterus. One doctor in London advocated against fiction, saying that "if a novel seemed to worsen a woman's condition, it should be taken away and replaced by 'a book upon some practical subject; such, for instance, as beekeeping.'"

I'd rather bee reading.

Develop enough courage
so that you can stand up
for yourself and

*then stand up
for someone
else.*

—Maya Angelou

What is right
to be done
cannot be done
too soon.

—Jane Austen

Pride + Prejudice

SENSE and SENSIBILITY

Mansfield Park

Persuasion

EMMA

Northanger Abbey

Literary Rivals

In Japan in the late 900s (its Heian period), two women contributed to the earliest Japanese writing and literature. Murasaki Shikibu and Sei Shōnagon, ladies-in-waiting and members of the royal court, were also literary rivals, according to Shikibu's own diaries.

fierce
fearless
female

Literary Rivals (cont'd)

Shikibu is best known for *The Tale of Genji*, considered to be the first modern novel.

The Pillow Book is a collection of lists, observations, gossip, poetry, and other musings written while Shōnagon lived at court serving Empress Teishi, also called Sadako.

Solving the Mystery of
Agatha Christie

The famous mystery writer...

...was a surfer.

...based the character Miss Marple on her grandmother.

...lived in Egypt because of her sick mother's need for a dry climate.

...disappeared for eleven days in 1926—and never revealed why.

"The best time to plan a book is while you're doing the dishes."

—Agatha Christie

The Queen of Crime Novels

According to Guinness World Records, Agatha Christie is the best-selling fiction writer of all time. She also once held the record for thickest book ever published for a collection of all of her Miss Marple stories.

AUTHOR	TITLE	DATE COMPLETED

Keep track of your reading—fill in this page and the bookmark with the titles of each book you've read!

AUTHOR	TITLE	DATE COMPLETED

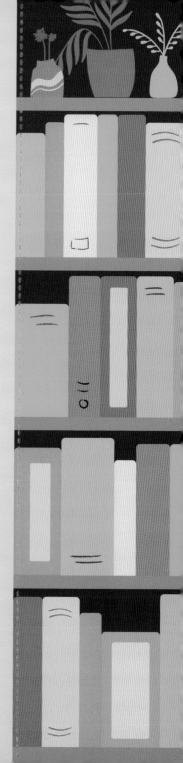

"WHERE THERE IS A WOMAN THERE IS *magic*."

—Ntozake Shange

Strong women

MAY WE BE THEM.
MAY WE READ THEM.
MAY WE WRITE THEM.

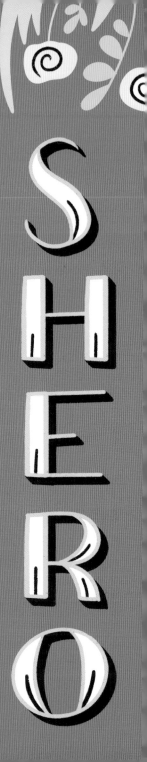

SHERO

"My candle burns at both ends;
It will not last the night;
But ah, my foes, and oh, my friends—
It gives a lovely light!"

—"First Fig," Edna St. Vincent Millay

Prolific Writers and Their Routines

George Sand wrote 20 pages (minimum) every single night, sometimes working into the wee hours.

Willa Cather did her writing in the morning for a couple of hours, then occupied herself with walks in New York City's Central Park, going to concerts, seeing friends, and staying fit.

Ayn Rand wrote day and night, hardly leaving her chair, and sometimes without going to bed for days.

Barbara Kingsolver, an early-morning writer, has said that she wakes "with sentences pouring into [her] head" and must get them onto the page as soon as possible.

Before she was published, Alice Munro wrote in the few moments she could spare between keeping house and raising children (saying she was "very big on naps").

SHE BELIEVED SHE COULD SO SHE wrote

"LIFE
Shrinks
OR
expands
ACCORDING TO ONE'S
COURAGE."

—Anaïs Nin

A Few Facts About
Louisa May Alcott

Before *Little Women*, Alcott wrote thriller short stories that she called "blood and thunder tales."

She was the first woman to register to vote in Concord, Massachusetts.

Alcott famously said she would rather be a "free spinster" than get married.

fortune favors THE bold.

FREEDOM

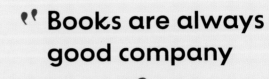

**Books are always
good company**

*if you have
the right sort.*"

—Louisa May Alcott, *Little Women*

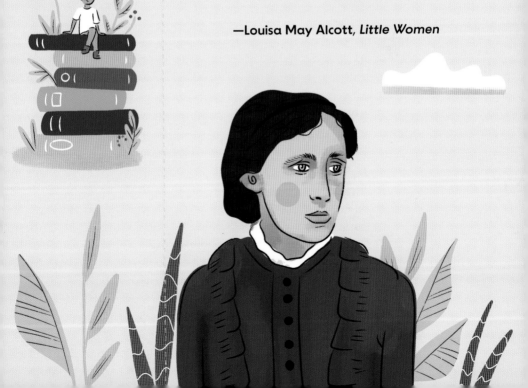

> WRITING IS AN EXTREME PRIVILEGE BUT IT'S ALSO A GIFT. IT'S A GIFT TO YOURSELF AND IT'S A GIFT OF GIVING A STORY TO SOMEONE.

—Amy Tan

Books: GIFTS YOU CAN OPEN AGAIN AND AGAIN

Portrait of a
Visionary Sci-fi Author

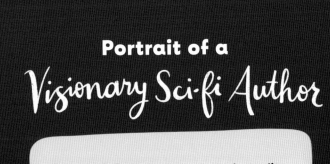

Octavia E. Butler spent so much quality time in libraries as a child that she knew what she wanted to be when she grew up: a writer. Not only did she get published, Butler became a Hugo and Nebula Award–winning science-fiction author. In 2021, NASA dubbed a landing spot for the Mars rover Perseverance the "Octavia E. Butler Landing" in her honor.

"In order to rise
From its own ashes
A phoenix
First
Must
Burn."

—Octavia E. Butler,
Parable of the Sower

"I BEGAN
WRITING
ABOUT
Power
BECAUSE
I HAD
SO LITTLE."

—Octavia E. Butler

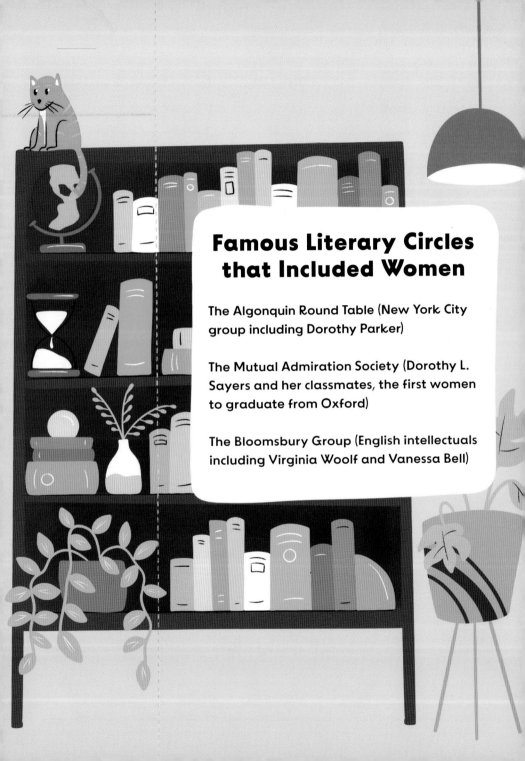

Famous Literary Circles that Included Women

The Algonquin Round Table (New York City group including Dorothy Parker)

The Mutual Admiration Society (Dorothy L. Sayers and her classmates, the first women to graduate from Oxford)

The Bloomsbury Group (English intellectuals including Virginia Woolf and Vanessa Bell)

TELEGRAM

JUNE 28, 1945

THIS IS INSTEAD OF TELEPHONING BECAUSE I CANT LOOK YOU IN THE VOICE. I SIMPLY CANNOT GET THAT THING DONE YET NEVER HAVE DONE SUCH HARD NIGHT AND DAY WORK NEVER HAVE SO WANTED ANYTHING TO BE GOOD AND ALL I HAVE IS A PILE OF PAPER COVERED WITH WRONG WORDS.

—excerpt from Dorothy Parker's telegram to her editor, June 28, 1945

WRITING IS NOT FOR THE faint of heart!